Additional Praise for *Cord Blood*

Bonnie Johnson-Bartee's poems in *Cord Blood* emerge from the grasslands of Nebraska where it takes work to nurture bounty. "Motherhood came hard as a spring thunderstorm," she writes, using birds and blossoms, cows and crops to frame stories of family. Across these pages, we see Johnson-Bartee's talent for using words in ways that reveal fresh meanings. In "Artistry," for example, nature infuses a baby with beauty: "each finger and toe an equinox bud" and the sound of a stream transforms into a visual design with a synesthetic use of scrimshaws. Sentences turn too, unveiling emotions; what begins as "The dance is a drunk-fest / filled with broken marriages," becomes the speaker worrying that she showed her daughter "how to love all wrong." Connecting the women in her family with the seasonal cycles of fertility and production that sustain her, the speaker of *Cord Blood* celebrates nature's power to heal. If you like earth under your nails and knee holes in your jeans, if you dream of being reborn as a wild rose in the grasslands, if you prefer quilts and the quiet hum of the heater as "winter whistles through naked trees," *Cord Blood* belongs in your hands.

Christine Stewart-Nuñez, South Dakota Poet Laureate 2019-2021,
The Poet & The Architect

Cord Blood

poems

BONNIE JOHNSON-BARTEE

SANDHILLS PRESS

Copyright ©2022 Bonnie Johnson-Bartee

All rights reserved. Printed in the United States of America. No part of this book may be used or reproduced in any manner whatsoever without the publisher's permission except in the case of brief quotations in critical articles or reviews.

Author Photo: Melinda Lewis Lowe

ISBN: 978-0-911015-87-6

FIRST EDITION

CONTENTS

MOTHER

Her Violet Fire ☞ 1
Justification ☞ 2
Artistry ☞ 3
Legacy ☞ 4
Intro to Politics ☞ 5
Divorced Mother of the Bride ☞ 6
Secret ☞ 7
Far, Far Away ☞ 8
Opposite of Comfortable ☞ 9
Master Drummer ☞ 11
Angel in Pink Flannel ☞ 12
Seconds ☞ 13
Heirloom Jewelry ☞ 15
Layers ☞ 16
I Taught my Daughter ☞ 17
Saint Rita, ☞ 18
Skitz ☞ 19
Re-used Frame ☞ 2
I See the Irony ☞ 21
Assessment ☞ 22
What a Girl Should Know ☞ 23

GRANDMOTHER

Relativity ☞ 27
Sarah and Chester Loved and Died ☞ 28
Heart of the Matter ☞ 29
Mulberry Tree ☞ 30
Cord Blood ☞ 31
Grandma's Wedding Ring ☞ 32
Writing in her Death Date ☞ 33
Yellow Umbrellas ☞ 34

Birthright ~ 35
Happy Endings ~ 36
Waning Crescent ~ 37
Lullaby ~ 38
Pre-School Prophetic ~ 39
Old Woman's Attic ~ 40
Cocoon ~ 41
Popcorn Pan ~ 42
Night Watch ~ 43
The Snapshot Is Darker ~ 44
One of Us ~ 45

EARTH MOTHER

A Stray ~ 49
Storm in the Heartland ~ 50
Mother of the Seasons ~ 51
Mulch ~ 52
Fowl ~ 53
A Little Plot of Plenty ~ 54
Red Finch, I Name Cherokee ~ 55
Cusp ~ 57
Pleas ~ 58
Nebraska Sun ~ 59
Pentobarbital ~ 60
Summons ~ 61
Twelve Foot Path of Destruction ~ 63
Wait ~ 64
Pedaling Notes ~ 65
Collective Unconscious ~ 66
Equinox ~ 67
Wandering Beauty ~ 68
Acknowledgments ~ 70
About the author ~ 71

For the women who are the bones of my family.

"We are together, my child and I. Mother and child, yes, but sisters really, against whatever denies us all that we are."

—Alice Walker (1944-)

Cord Blood

MOTHER

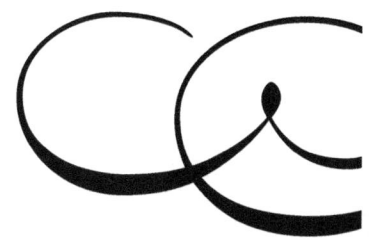

Her Violet Fire

Fists of embers,
fire goddesses' embrace
fuels all -- fertility to death.
Full circle they dance hand-in-hand
to a single beat of a collective drum
around the licking blaze.

A snare of fire,
sharp teeth of ashes --
puberty, childbirth, mothering,
her soft seeds wither and die
inside over-ripe fruit,
audience to

Pele, Nantosuelta, Ida
chanting their overture
of devotion, family, nature.
They bow, rise, writhing lightning,
ageless hymn to the precursor
of death -- her new birthing.

The finale, her aria,
mystery of flames and energy,
lost in unwavering revelation of wonder.
In the heat of high soprano,
she sings, simmers,
shimmers with the perspiration of readiness.

Justification

Sweat from the glass
trickles onto her jeans,
a denim coaster
soaking up summer.

At the pub
it would be cardboard
ripped piece by piece,
small piles of trash
fingers push around on the bar.

Much how she feels
as she stares at her 7&7
through Momma's eyes.
Always a great time
until it isn't.

A battle of wills
hyphenated by sobs,
punctuated with welts. . .

She goes home
when she needs a reason
to have one more
past too many.

Artistry

Nature painted you, daughter,
with creamy peach skin,
blushing air-brushed lips,
August-bleached blue eyes,
and solar-blonde hair.

She sketched your tiny body,
each finger and toe an equinox bud,
and plump, curving infant hips and thighs
from rolling Nebraska plains.

She drew your laughter
from giggling aquifer streams,
innocence scrimshawed
by emergent springs.

She shaded your temper
with hues of October leaves, April tornados,
and carefully crafted your heart
from the sweet winter blues.

My sweet girl,
your breath
inhales the wide grassy pastures,
exhales the starry summer sky.
You are a glory to behold.

Legacy

Rubies,
polished by years of mistakes, acceptance,
passed down from Great Grandma Zegers, Grandma Sehi,
and my beautiful mother Joan,
we are all one woman, Eve,
mirror of many faces,
each unique, loved, treasured
myself,
my daughter,
and hers.

Seasoned with smile lines
and gray hair
earned through hard years,
I've learned

age is a powerful tool --
beauty
replaced with a mellow glow of peace.
After many loves and losses,
I still have a big heart,
have learned pleasing others
isn't as important as doing what's right.
I can stick to my morals
and my faults.
Beauty isn't judged by clothes, make-up
or weight.
And my children
play their role in humanity
will not just be a part of it.

I am proud of this legacy,
the soft femininity and solidity of womanhood,
a unity of sisters
        on our Mother Earth.

Intro to Politics

Summer Sunday night,
Mom's oven roast, scalloped potatoes, and corn-on-the-cob.
Betty, George, and I take turns with ice and salt, crank dessert.
Dad's home early from poker at the VFW,
a five spot in his t-shirt pocket for each of us.
Omaha's Wild Kingdom at six, *Disney* at seven.

Belly full, I snuggle down on the green vinyl couch,
wrapped in a quilt, palming a bowl of ice-cream, spoon in hand.
Music plays, fireworks erupt in black and white over the castle,
Flipper begins.

Silver dolphin, Sandy, Florida Keys, a harpoon . . .
Then Walter Cronkite,
President Nixon.
We change channels,
but the president's on all three.

Bowl and spoon in the kitchen sink, I head for my treehouse,
but Mom hollers.
I pretend not to hear and keep walking.
Bonnie Sue Johnson, get in the tub!

Grandma was right,
There's always somebody bigger.

Divorced Mother of the Bride

She was seven
when she found my wedding dress
dry-cleaned and sealed
in the dark spare bedroom closet.

She wanted to try it on,
twirl in the mirror,
dream of Prince Charming.
No.
Marriage isn't a game.

Now twenty-one
she's choosing her wedding gown,
trying on white silk, cream taffeta,
playing dress-up with her happiness.

A mother's wordless fears
and her daughter's breathless dreams
wrapped together
in new nuptial paper
decorated with a tattered ribbon.

Secret

Sunflowers were my father's,
are my daughter's favorite.
But she doesn't know
she shares this love
for those solar yellow buds
straining for August blue,
that I favor them, glorious,
in eager summer abandon.

Her knowledge of our link
would lead to its dismissal.

Old wives have told
by the bursting ditches of lush clusters
this will be a hard winter.
Flowers with an exaggerated growth plate,
their height as yet a secret
forecast deep wet piles of snow,
cold as the heart of a teenage girl
toward her mother.

Stiff necks hold seeds high
and gather warmth,
storing strength for blue-black February.

Far, Far Away

One day when the temp forecast was over 90,
she didn't refill the dogs' dishes or the birdbath,
water the flowers or the grass seed she'd planted two days before.
She ate two bowls of cereal, didn't take her vitamins,
didn't brush her teeth, just rinsed and spat.

She called in sick after her husband left for work,
and sat in the recliner all day watching bad Lifetime movies,
drinking wine laced with Oxy leftover from last year's surgery.
Her cellphone rang unanswered.
The dogs pissed on the rug by the door.

She napped.

Get-your-own supper night
turned to Facebook games.
Hubby went to bed, angry and alone.
Late in the night, she still couldn't sleep,
so she daydreamed of running.

Opposite of Comfortable

All girlie-girl
in hundred-percent hand-made
mother-of-the-bride
dusty rose silk,
poofy hair and polished nails,
welcoming family
I've never met.
Scared eyes
over a gracious-pink lipstick smile
hide choked-up tears
one kind word from falling.

I watch my ex-husband
with his obnoxious girlfriend
dance to our song,
the groom's mom hugging her husband
while his dad does shots
with his new blonde,
and I think
about all the left-overs.

The dance is a drunk-fest
filled with broken marriages,
whiskey and rum to forget.
We're all here to celebrate an innocent beginning,
but I'm terrified
I showed her how to love all wrong.

My little girl dances in the white
cloak of a woman's vow,
and I pray,
over AC/DC and The Village People,
she stays happy as she is right now.

Painful two-and-a-half-inch cream heels
orphaned on the DJ's speaker,
I rub my pantyhose-clad toes,
a sad try for some small comfort.

Master Drummer

Her long slender hands, self-manicured
corals and pinks held the sticks.
Rhythm rapid and choppy,
six-pack deep and six bars long.
My chorus of cries and pleas went unheard.
She played to her own beat –
one of tradition, deep in muscle memory.

I too played.
My children's voices an echo of past concerts
as tiny bodies stretched and arched in pain.
Tender hands reach to cover battered bruises.
Shells on the edge of breaking
under habit's heavy weight.

From somewhere deep in the beat
their chorus ricocheted
and their singing grew louder.
The snare silenced,
the pattern ended.

Angel in Pink Flannel

No denying the harsh assault
and sterile smell
of white floors and walls, under one hundred and twenty-watt lights.
My right hand traces the railing,
winding through corridors to find her.

A quiet knock
and I peek through the barely open door.
My eyes catch his,
the fear of the last twenty-four hours
abating now, like sobs,
after his wife's fruitless labor.
The ancient ritual gone wrong.
My stomach contracts.

But cradled in his arms, an infant
freshly scalpelled from the womb,
now swaddled in soft white flannel.
He offers me his firstborn,
but I turn
to my daughter.
She's vulnerable, weak,
wrapped in starched white sheets and a pink flannel blanket.
I reach for her.

Seconds

With all four leaves
the table that seats fourteen
is surrounded by twenty and two highchairs.
Oak decorated with child-proof battery candles, crystal glasses,
Bud Light bottles, sippy cups, and a golden turkey on a silver tray.
Family packed arm-to-arm and belly-up
with five more young ones at the kid table
positioned on vinyl for spills.
Last year the family pet, Sparky,
weaved between dangling feet, cleaning the floor.
But this year he's gone, buried
by the lilac bushes in the back yard.

Mom's soon-to-be second husband, Charley,
says the Thanksgiving prayer,
and it's long,
really long.

Betty and I look at each other, heads bowed,
hands folded, but eyes raised.
I stray a glance at my daughter
who's looking at me,
and we grin. But the turkey is cooling,
and she's pregnant and hungry.
Grandkids start to fuss,
and a tiny hand reaches for a pickle,
but her mom pulls it back.
A cell phone rings
a slot-machine jingle,
and the hushed giggles are contagious.

Maybe he gets the hint, and *Amen* sounds,
and dishes of lukewarm food pass like batons,
as silence falls around the table,
and around again for seconds
until talk of poker and pitch, NASCAR, and Nebraska football
signal full bellies.

Heirloom Jewelry

My troubles line up
like pearls.
Caressed between thumb
and first finger,
I rub them clean.
Filth falls away and they gleam
opalescent.
I hold the string taut,
one
by
one
eye them closely
and count them off,
a rusty rosary of prayers that never work.

Layers

Off-white, pine-green, Mobile blue,
four-year-old tan chipped paint
framing heavy black screen.

Annually washed clean
of cottonwood seeds, box-elders,
fly shit, wind-driven dirt.

Years sieved
with each slam.
> *Mom, I'm home!*
> *What's for supper?*
> *Guess what?*

Everything now
new-fangled security
and air-tight silence.

This house is much too quiet
for an old lady, waiting.

I Taught my Daughter

to brush her teeth
for the length of the ABCs
and to keep her shoulders square.
Cut toenails straight across
so they don't get in-grown
and wipe from front to back.
Knock on a cantaloupe
and reach in the back
for the freshest milk.
Use hospital corners
when changing sheets
and hammer a nail dead-on straight.
Use dark red kidney beans
and a can of tomato soup in chili
and only real butter on hot homemade bread.
How to do simple fractions
with an old angel food cake recipe
and the importance of a consistent signature.
Fill the hole with Miracle Grow
when planting vegetables
and never water the flowers in afternoon sun.

But I couldn't teach what I didn't know,
and I taught her how to love all wrong.

Saint Rita,

> *of impossible and desperate causes,*
> *please help my daughter.*

Cowering in her ex's crosshairs,
she bows
behind a blonde cascade.

Camouflaged with faux strength,
she wears fleece-lined silk
cloaked with invisibility,
concealing her flayed confidence.

She prays
for the solar flares of rage
to condense, diffuse to vapor.

Stuck in her throat, she chokes
on death-do-you-part guilt,
funeral vows.

Untended soul, seeds
moldering in dead dirt.
Oblivious to compassion,
she waits alone.

Tears lodge behind swollen eyes, dammed
by faith, friends, family.
This road, Saint Rita, is harder than rock.

Skitz

Like master of chaos, Picasso,
she laughs or smiles
a pretty picture,

but a shot glass of thinner
runs down her face
and shatters into colorful shards.

Disorder screams in violets
hidden behind the soft blues
of confusion in bloodshot eyes,
her self-portrait.

James, Patron Saint,
holds a pistol and a syringe,
vessels of shimmering escape.

She flings blood-red paint
at the flaming walls
on the stairway to her manic mind.

Re-used Frame

She stands tip-toe to reach
a picture on the shelf,
brings it eye level,
blows off loose dust,
then wipes glass with her stained white shirt.
A gold-framed foreshadowing.

> Her daughter at the altar,
> satin, lace, and pearls.
> Soft ringlets frame a tanned face,
> white smile.
> Sparkling blue eyes hint.

The picture is clear now.
Not that she could've stopped the boulder
rolling down, picking up speed.

She walks to the kitchen table,
takes a sip of coffee, knows it will burn.
Deserves it.
Turns the picture over,
loosens the tiny screws to free her daughter.

Then places the image face-down,
takes the top photo from a new envelope,
her son and his soon-to-be bride.
She searches his face.

I See the Irony

I let my granddaughter challenge bedtime,
scheme for brownies and orange popsicles,
create *It wasn't me* stories of fairies and wind,
watch butterflies shuffle through remnants of dreams,
Crayola to the edge and beyond.

I stopped my daughter with spankings,
answered questions right
so she wouldn't remember them wrong,
washed away 6:00 a.m. sleep with a rough sour rag,
eliminated defiance with *Bad girl*, *Naughty*,
ripped her doll away,
pushed curiosity back inside the lines.

Assessment

It's funny
how in my eyes
Mom never aged
after 1973 --

Aqua Net-glued, Cover Girl dark-ash beehive,
black horn-rimmed glasses,
Lee jeans belly-button high,
Jane Russell bra and a tight sweater --

but today,
she looks like Grandma.
It's time I look in the mirror.

What a Girl Should Know

Mom tried to teach me all levels of girlish propriety --
Yes, ma'am and *Yes, sir,*
to not talk back,
or cuss,
remember prayers
and respect my elders.

But I was a tomboy,
climbed the oak tree in the neighbor's yard,
painted myself with mulberries,
scavenged through the trash for treasures,
played with baby bunnies,
built forts in the shelter belt.

No time for prayers
and less for her liver and onions on Mondays.
I knew well the taste of Dial
and had many spankings.
I liked the earth under my nails and knee holes in my jeans.
Dresses and church made me itch.

But we survived, and a long while later,
during a Friday night and some Bud Lights,
we spilled memories at the table,
and she let it slip

that her folks stowed her
away in the virgin Sandhills
at the ripe age of thirteen
to be a nun-in-training.

But Joanie was a tomboy,

missed prayers,
laughed too loud after lights-out,
yawned during mass,
hated the starched uniform,
talked back to Mother Superior,
and got herself kicked out of that convent.

It took me forty-three years to find out
what a girl should really know about her mom.

GRANDMOTHER

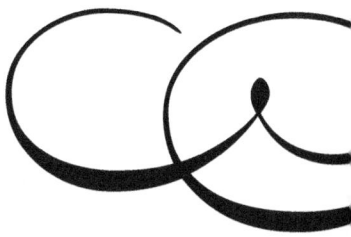

Relativity

I never met Cleo.
It's hard to call her Grandma.

I've seen only one photo,
in an oval oak frame with beveled glass,
a black and white studio of her in her wedding gown.

I have the same nose and cheekbones
both higher than normal.

County fair ribbons say she made the best
angel food cake in Antelope County,
but the recipe is lost.

I wonder what she would think of me --
a poet, a teacher,
not a Methodist or Republican.

I'm sure her voice was soft and calming,
that she loved working with her hands in gardens,
that she tucked the children in and sang lullabies.

I wonder if I have her gene for breast cancer
that took her life at thirty-three.
I wonder what she thought when she heard the news
and looked at four children – two to fourteen.

As I search those quiet, dark eyes,
frozen in a blink of 1920's history,
I wish I could comfort her.

Sarah and Chester Loved and Died

Between these stones is a story
of survival in the Sandhills
passed around Thanksgiving tables,
like mashed potatoes to hungry children.

Great-great grandma's quilt,
frayed, sun-bleached Levi's
and brick-red flannel
bound with sack-cloth skirts,
stitched with simple, deliberate strokes.

Her forty-six-piece white china,
bought with egg money, piano lessons
and seamstress work, piece-at-a-time
through the Sears catalog.

His Hawthorn walking stick,
polished with linseed oil in years of plenty
and lard during leaner,
the beauty of its wood a cruel mimicking of the crippled hands
that wore it smooth.

The Henry repeater was an education
aimed at whiskey bottles and tin cans,
that taught compassion and necessity,
downed prairie chickens and rabbits.

They lie together in Cedarview,
under sinking stones green with moss,
decorated with prairie grass,
nestled among family.

Heart of the Matter

They'd been married forty-seven years
and him dead fifteen more
before I asked how they met.

Albert was a young farmer, Erma a school girl,
and he was sweet on her.
But she had plans
to be a nanny in California,
and he was too shy to ask her
to stay in Clearwater
to be his wife.
So she left.

Bravery grew from loneliness
and he sent word to San Francisco --
her father was dying,
she was needed at home.

She returned to find her father
working the fields,
and herself too broke to go back.

Then here he came
in his Sunday suit,
with a wilted red carnation pinned to his lapel,
spit-shined work boots,
cocky and proud,
Albert riding his tall red roan
up the lane, straight to the house.

Mad, she made him grovel,
apologize,
get on his knee
before she said *Yes*.

Mulberry Tree

Smack-dab in the middle
of Gramps' *No Trespassing* pasture,
it squatted with limbs low and inviting.
Deep-purple juice
stained play clothes, bare feet, pink lips.

We sat in her heavy arms,
talked with indigo tongues
about the Fonz, 4th grade, and boys,
as young calves slept in the sun
and suckled their mommas.

Renee laughed too loud,
like she always did, and pretty soon
Gramps crested the west hill
in his faded-blue '62 Chevy
and yelled from the fence line,
Get outta there before you scare them cows!

We dropped from the tree like ripe fruit
with the Cool Whip bowls
she'd given us to fill,
and ran straight for Grandma,
and sugar,
and cream.

Cord Blood

Another 4 a.m. phone call
but this time I'm ready,
sleeping with my mind open.
My sister says, *Grandma . . .*
I say, *. . .is gone.*
I felt it happen,
the baton passed to my mother
in my wide-awake dream.

Mid-April Nebraska morning,
I stand at the edge of a blue, snapping tent
staked in the Clearwater sand at St. John's,
chilled by the sun playing with shadows.

Mom sits on a velvet chair reserved for family,
too weak and tired
to bear the heavy load of matriarchy.
We stand, bow and pray.

My daughter, swollen with female child,
holds a fragrant red rose,
as does my mother,
as does my sister,
as do I.

One-by-one, we place each on the silver-gold casket.
Our heirloom of love within.
Standing together – one family of women,
cord blood flowing through our woven hands –
we let her go
back to the womb.

Grandma's Wedding Ring

When Grandpa was just Daddy,
my momma and four siblings still tender,
he hammered a ten-penny in the oak crosshead of the marriage room.

Mom remembers looking up at that ring.
It still hangs in her mind, a token of --

Faith --
A family of seven piles into the '46 Chevy sedan for Sunday services at St. John's.
Clasped hands frame a supper table of fried chicken, potatoes and gravy.
Knees bent on cold hardwood floors at 9 p.m. bedtime.

Learning --
Patience through February all-nighters waiting for heifers to calve.
Mathematics and manners with bacon and eggs at the kitchen table.
Rocking chair and a full lap, *Black Beauty* through low light and cherry pipe smoke.

Hope --
Fingers knuckle-deep in moist, sandy soil, urging white daisies and yellow mums.
Egg money stored in the sugar jar for a Saturday night dance at Two Rivers.
Fragile tomato seedlings in egg cartons, sunning on the window sill.

Albert and Erma's marriage
left a golden heritage. Dutch and German values
rang like windchimes in an April breeze
and still echo across the family farm.

Writing in her Death Date

One crisp May morning after Gramma passed,
they found a black-n-white photo
dated back
to a long damn time ago
carefully placed in the family-tree leaves
of her King James Bible.

Mom and Uncle Jack stood side-by-side,
each holding a corner
of the yellowed, scalloped-paper frame,
scanning the faces for recognition
in pronounced cheekbones,
high hair line, mis-positioned curve of an upper lip.

Seventeen people, sitting or standing, all crammed together
on a stagecoach, smiling at the camera,
heading somewhere
they eventually found
since this is home.

Yellow Umbrellas

Motherhood came hard as a spring thunderstorm.
Spent my time watching the radar,
riding it out in the cellar,

I emerged,
graying like the wood of a weathered barn,
kissed with grandchildren
who bathe me in color.

A renewal I didn't expect --
to see the difference between magenta and pink,
find fuzz in belly buttons,
watch *Bambi* and cry,
run through the tall grass and straight to the river,
catch minnows with butterfly nets
and tiny frogs with snow-cone cups.
Find boats, bicycles, and fire engines in the clouds,
sing London Bridge and laugh when we all fall down,
fill up on popcorn before supper,
stay up late telling ghost stories,
and laugh at root beer belches.

I itch with regret
it took me so long to get it right.
I should've played in the rain all along.

Birthright

I wake in the night
weeping
for my granddaughter

growing in a patch of Nebraska farmland
where generations have pillaged the earth
and left
emptiness
laced with chemicals,
steroids, sewage,
greed.

It's not her fault.
But it's become
her punishment.

Happy Endings

Her baby-fine hair
snarls in the bristles
of the brush.
A few more squirts of detangler
and shorter strokes, but she cries.

So I tell a story
of fairies
and a princess just like her,
and a kind queen in a faraway land.
I weave, add in a playful mouse
and a cunning fox. She laughs.
I braid, pull it all together
into a clean, perfect tale.

Waning Crescent

Her beautiful smallness bathed in moonlight,
wrapped in her green kitty blanket,
her arm curled around her stuffed pony,
eyelids flickering
like clapboard scenes in her dreams.

I fear, somewhere between
footie pajamas and the evening news,
with the frustration and futility
that adults slam into young minds,
society will harden her trust,
pulverize her innocence.

Lullaby

She's supposed to be taking a nap,
but Grandma's here
and Mom's not.
On this cold rainy May Tuesday
we huddle by the window in her parents' bedroom,
watch her daddy and grandpa work the cows and calves.
Her butt rests on shoeboxes, sippy cup in one hand,
dolly and her bottle with disappearing orange juice in the other.

Gamma Bonnie, what's Daddy doing?
Separating the cows and calves.
Why?
Because the babies need to eat grass now; they're getting big.
Why?
They can't suckle their mommies anymore, like when your mommy took your bottle away.
She looks at her dolly's bottle, *Why?*
'Cause babies get big. See, you're drinking out of a sippy cup.
Why?
Because. That's how it works.

She sinks through the stacked cardboard,
untangles, squeals, bolts out of the room. Slower to rise, I follow.
Okay, little one, it's naptime.
No! Blonde hair dancing as she streaks through the living room.
And no sippy cup at naptime anymore, remember?
Blue eyes and a tiny nose peek around the couch.
Am I getting big?
Yes, sweetheart, you are.

I reach down and lift her small body into my arms.
Her head on my chest,
she falls asleep to the lullaby of bawling calves.

Pre-School Prophetic

My granddaughter looks through her fairy-dust blues
straight into my crows-feet-lined eyes
and gives fresh kindergarten wisdom:
You get what you get, and you don't throw a fit!

Old Woman's Attic

We stare at each other
in an ornate, oval mirror
bought at a thrift store
for twenty dollars,
found in an attic
of an old widow's home.

My eyes stray from my reflection
to my granddaughter's
blue eyes, peach cheeks,
childish lines. Her small body a promise,
full of new seeds,
ready to flower.

She finds my wrinkles funny,
and I'm honored,
because here with me
she has yet to earn her own.

Cocoon

By April my energy is sapped,
meetings, parents, and donuts on the go.
I drag what's left of me through May.
When the bells chime Pomp and Circumstance,
I wrap myself in a cocoon of summer,
in strong silk filament of flowers,
dogs and vegetable gardens.
The sun bronzes my skin,
lightens my hair.
I shed the weight of routine,
read novels until late,
sleep until noon.
Days upon days of innocent chats
with grandchildren,
lunch dates of grape popsicles
and grape tomatoes.
At last, arms spread wide,
I dance with the wind.

Popcorn Pan

The neighbor kids and we
played Monopoly on snow-days,
inhaled buttery kernels
fistful at a time, trading Boardwalk
for North Carolina and Pacific Avenue.
George spilled grease,
hot from a fresh batch,
on the threadbare green carpet,
couldn't hide the smell of burnt plastic.

Mom and I watched
the *Roots* broadcast premier
night after night
alone with each other
and a metal bowl popcorn-warm.
Nestled on the green couch
covered with worn-out afghans
fingers rubbing the tasseled ends.

My teeth snapped off sharp hulls
to leave fluffy white kernels
for my infant daughter to enjoy
without choking. On standby
an old green Tupperware cup, complete
with sippy lid, full of milk to wash it down.

Friday nights spent with Mom,
kids, half-grown grandkids
belly up to a table lined
with Kool-Aid, Mountain Dew, Bud Light
around a heaping bowl of popcorn,
fresh from the 1½-quart steel pan
caked with years
that'll never wear out.

Night Watch

Restful sleep to a mind-blowing howl,
no tears,
her wide blue eyes glaze
with a fear held by the small dams of her lids.

Pulling her close, chest-to-chest,
Grandma curls her hands around the tender body
that writhes in spasms and struggles for breaths.
Poor baby. Now now, Grandma has you sweetheart.

Their hearts thump, separate, powerful.
The more calloused, slow and steady,
the younger
falling into rhythm
like a puppy to a clock.

Heavy sobs occasional as hiccups
shake her body as she returns to the dream.
The rocker pulls an all-nighter.

The Snapshot Is Darker

Only five
and a yardstick high,
weighing less than a 50-cent piece.
Bedhead curls licked with static,
and those hazel eyes
pooling with first-day kindergarten tears.
Her sparkly purple unicorn backpack
full of paper, pencils, kleenex, blunt scissors,
and brand-spanking-new compliance.

Color in the lines.
Raise your hand to speak.
Shame on you. No recess.
Sit still!
No, not another bathroom break until lunch.
Hurry up and eat.

She's so damn cute,
I stop to take a picture.

One of Us

My granddaughter walks up the aisle
in a beautiful white dress, lace veil.
Flanked by divorced parents.
It's only first communion,
but her future is fated
if the pattern follows suit.

From the back pew
I watch this child play dress-up bride,
a come-to-Jesus ruse.
Jaded to religion,
I flinch from the holy water
the priest sprinkles on the crowd.

Still there's Mary.
She escaped my hatred
for this banter and circumstance.
Her statue stands left of the altar,
a death grip on her son.
I lost one too.
At one time, we were both
unpopular, early, un-wed moms.

She suffered sleepless nights
of teething, feedings,
colds. She changed dirty diapers,
kissed banged-up knees,
scraped hands, stubbed toes.

It's a comfort
that we'll both be watching.

EARTH MOTHER

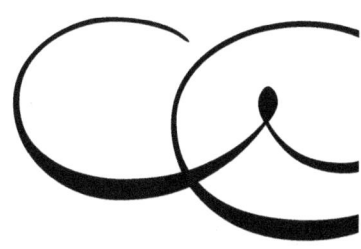

A Stray

"We must bloom where we are planted." *Call the Midwife*

A magnificent treasure chest --
rubies, gold coins, pearls,
diamonds as large as a fist --
always out of reach
just off the edge of the map.

Shoulders rolled forward, head down,
wading through streams,
digging around trees older than my family name.

Whether happenstance or exhaustion
or both,
a rock jumped in front of my blind foot
and I tripped, twisted,
landed on my back.

But I see the stars and the sun
the way the leaves dance with the breeze,
a kaleidoscope of lilies and violets.
I feel the soft moss under my tired body,
the kiss of June warmth.
I arch to the scent of the far-off ocean,
the mustiness of fresh earth.
I hear the song of robins,
the secret whispers of the forest.

Holding still,
I drink in all I've missed,
all I've robbed myself of
in the search for riches.

Storm in the Heartland

A cold Coors and a burning Macanudo
on the porch while I watch
the storm's overture.
Blue sits at my feet
and pants heavy breath.
Humidity hangs from the gutters.

One… two… three…
thunder rattles the windows.
According to Grandma,
the storm's three miles away.

The hanging flowers and pots
are snug to the house,
the peas are laced,
tomatoes tied,
but I'll just keep my fingers crossed
for the beans, onions and peppers,
flower beds,
this year's saplings.

One… two….
northwest wind cracks with thunder,
the neighbor's old Maple sweeps low
then snaps back.
Rain drops splat on the steps,
then like a drum roll,
a chorus of thunder, lightning and cool gusts,
and rain,
thank God for the rain.
The show begins.

Mother of the Seasons

She arrives early.
Pecks at the frost line
to urge fishing bait up.

The robin lifts, flies, perches in an oak
hundreds of years older
than she,
sees
where to build her shelter
before the next migration
spreads
north,
south
and again.

Mulch

On days like this
the soft March breezes
bring faint hints of Old Spice,
airplane paint, gunpowder,
whiskey, cigarette smoke,
shoe polish and sweat.

Something about the birth of spring
re-kindles the ashes
of the dead
in me.

Fowl

> "Everything is just as it was everywhere else."
> Leo Tolstoy, *War and Peace*

Each morning,
like Eirene,
I walk to the backyard, carrying seed and suet,
hands full of compassion,
a joining, an olive branch.

Surrounded by fenced-in wildflowers,
the birdfeeders hang peacefully at sunrise.
They dangle from shepherds' crooks,
like uninhabited countries.

Once full, they come alive
with red-breasted finches,
robins, plain sparrows, cooing doves.
Eager to eat, willing to play fair.

Pigeons land at the base,
too heavy to balance, too large to care.
Then the starlings, warriors of greed,
scare off others, fight amongst themselves.
Feathers and feed fly at the trough,
ruthless beaks spear fragile bodies
spiral down, up, levitate on magic talons.
Their war cry sounds of an army
willing to die in order to win.

The displaced perch on roof tops,
garage doors, the neighbor's fence,
a bird's eye view, wait for the bloodbath to end
and pray for leftovers.
But the pigeons still forage,
pay no heed.

A Little Plot of Plenty

In this land of box-top rooftops,
patchwork fences, and bottleneck yards,
it's tough to forage enough land
to stake a claim.

It feels good to grow
without pesticides,
herbicides.
A few flags, bit of string,
an envelope or two of seeds.
Plots in good black dirt.

On knees, she weeds past small plants,
prays for rain, and wipes sweat.
She bets on spades, and hoes the rows,
a taste of what it took
before Walmart's organic aisle.

Lettuce, tomatoes, taters and beans.
Gallons
and gallons of beans.
More than she can eat.
Facebook posts, phone calls,
still the fridge overflows,
turns a crisper to a coffin
and wilts
mulch for next season.

Red Finch, I Name Cherokee

We eye each other
through the pane door.
This red finch and I
have done countless dances.
She spreads her wings, swoops,
and I bend, bow,
both afraid,
caught between escape and protect.
It's my porch,
her nesting ground.

***

A flock of breakfast noise,
the chirping of hungry young,
Keurig hums, pans bang.
The red finch flies
back and forth,
prods earth to give life,
exhaustive repetition of sacrifice and prayer.
And she's so proud.
Perched on the open door,
she sings
This is my land,
my children.

***

Just like that the singing stops.
Our fledglings gone.

Busy with loneliness,
she flies in to check her empty nest.
I water the pansies and marigolds,
see her by the feeder.
Familiar now with grief, removal,
our trail ends.

Cusp

*Foggy mornings slide into fall
scrape elbows with winter.*

Sheltered by cottonwoods
and lilac bushes
long past their bloom,
a stray songbird
safe for the moment
listens to the collective hum
of cicadas.
This time,
a southern flight just too far.

Pleas

Seeking comfort deep in the night
with heavy quilt
and quiet hum of heater,
winter whistling through naked trees,

I rub her swollen belly,
work my way to velvet ears,
down bony spine,
and back to soft tummy,

spanning my fingers,
a healer, anointing.

I bargain with God,
with the Devil,
for a kinder place than this,

and that I'm not forced to make that choice.
That she finds her call back to the wild
in painless dreams.

Nebraska Sun

She cycles
with me past sunflowers, rivers,
open pastures.
She bakes me
a soft caramel,
cheeks and nose kissed pink.
I seal her heat,
before the season's pop.
Her tan warms me through winter.

Pentobarbital

for my Tessa Marie

My lap is heavy with my talisman
of the last fifteen years.
Almost dead-weight now.

Energy flows blue,
flits like a gold butterfly,
twilight vapor condensing into clouds.

Brown and blue eyes magically coalesce,
souls meander
to a pinpoint.

Injected silvery pearls
flow through marrow and mind,
the treasure of suspended time,
find the inheritance
of relief.

We go separate ways
for the first sad
and glorious time.

Summons

A screaming chorus
summons me to the patch
below the skeletal elm.

Tangled in strawberry netting
a small robin,
feathers like wrinkled clothes
stick legs and talons
crochet hooked in a chaotic pattern,
thin spindle neck at a hard-right angle.

Thought she was dead,
but her right eye watches
as I crouch low.
Out of black fear, the instinct to flee,
she struggles,

then goes limp,
no choice but to trust
my scissors
snip --
snipping
her leg free.
I wait on the wings,
afraid of damage.

Her pale chest heaves,
beak part open,
neck wound tight,
wings bound
in layers of woven squares.

The final cut,
her wings free,
she stumbles and beats
ground to air
ground to air
to tree.

Standing, I wonder
when the chorus stopped.

Twelve Foot Path of Destruction

Each spring our lawn bounds
back plush and green,
but a twelve-foot path plays dead,
belly up, waiting for a good rub.

It winds from the patio steps
across the yard,
then like a braided rope through the lilac row,
six inches wide.
It begs for treats
of seed, fertilizer, rain.

We dig up patches of weeds,
fetch fresh sod.
Roll over the dirt to give it a chance
then circle with sprinkles of bluegrass
before lying it down,
like carefully planted bones.

Then to find a kiss of shade,
let it enjoy the slow drool of the soaker hose
through the lazy days of summer.

Wait

Heavy with the weight of waking,
Spring lays her neck back, reaches with the stretch of a long sleep,
runs fingers through matted bedhead,
ponders a trim, a shower,

pulls back the heavy maple quilt,
revealing a full womb,
promise of blossoms and do-overs,
rises with a rush of warmth,
and with her head in the clouds, sings.

Pedaling Notes

I head south to face the music,
to break from the city
lights and sounds that dull my center.
Cycle miles
deep into summer-blue Nebraska sky country
embraced by hills of oak and cottonwood
that sing if I listen.
Red-winged blackbirds follow, shadows
on concrete's rippling-heat,
swoop and dance. My friends.
An audience of old cows stand at the fence
and chew. I nod. Gear down,
prepare for a hill. Pasture grass leans forward,
the breeze urges me on.
Rhythm and harmony of a meadowlark,
occasional oriole.
The creek teems with dragonflies
and the throaty songs of frogs.
The sun,
a spotlight directed solely on me,
heals.

Miles
before my mind is quiet enough
to turn around,
return home to face the noise.

Collective Unconscious

> "There is no fundamental difference between man and animals in their ability to feel pleasure and pain, happiness, and misery."
> — Charles Darwin

Stuck at a red light
on Norfolk's fast-food highway,
I lock the eye of a steer
in a hot cattle pot.
I can see the fear,
feel his adrenalin
run through my veins.

He knows. Has always known.
The nervous bellers still
hang in the stagnant air
of the feedlot.

If only
he had a chance
to flee his fate
ten miles south
at the packing plant.
Smell of slaughter
before it comes, blood
flowing around his hooves,
circling down the drain
as he waits,
locked in a chute with no escape.

I can't look away,
the memory embedded deep.
Then the trailer rocks and lunges forward
for the last leg of his journey.

Equinox

Spring rubs her eyes,
eases the heavy quilt off her body,
inches her legs over the side of the bed
and reaches for the sun in a full sitting-stretch,

hair tousled and bobbed,
rosy cheeks aglow with sleep,
still indecisive
whether to hit the snooze once, twice,
or rise to her feet and begin the day.

Wandering Beauty

Growing season
to growing season
her hands knead moist soil,
pinch seeds,
pluck peas, dig potatoes,
pull beets, carrots
for family
now grown and gone
to garden on their own.

She kneels on the body
of Mother,
the one to whom she prays
to keep her seedlings safe
from evil clouds
and droughts.
It clears the dust.

She rests more after fifty years,
alternates crops and flowers,
rockers herself, waits through
the rest of winter to regenerate.
She knows patience

learned through hard years
of deep-set weeds. Painful,
dirty process. Nails break,
tips bleed, hurt seeps into soil,
absorbs, reincarnates.
Phoenix, she sinks
and rises.

Her life full of even rows
and schedules,
she hopes to be reborn a wild rose
high on the untended Sandhills' grassland,
free to scatter her petals on a soft breeze,
a wandering beauty,
blushing red in the full sun
of an August sky.

Acknowledgments

Sincerest gratitude to my friend and mentor, Neil Harrison, for his encouragement and education. You are an amazing human being, sir. Thank you for believing in me. Cheers to countless more days of wine, horseradish, Keno, and conversation.

Many thanks to my writing group friends for their insight: Neil Harrison, JV Brummels, Grizz McIntosh, Maureen Kingston, Tana Buoy, Barbara Schmitz, Karen Wingett, Lin Brummels, and Jen Ippensen.

Appreciation for the support my husband, Jimmy, gave me during the development of this book. #hoty

Finally, to the women who made everything possible, the mothers and grandmothers, daughters and granddaughters: thank you for the inspiration, for the humanness that links us.

Bonnie Johnson-Bartee is the author of two chapbooks of poetry, *Bildungsroman 38* (2004) and *Named, but Unknown* (2006), and is the editor of *Teachers College: Essays on the Art of Education* (WSC Press, 2007). Her work can be found in *Words Like Rain* (WSC Press, 2005) and editions of *Voices Out of Nowhere* and *Judas Goat*. She teaches creative writing and literature courses at Wayne State College in Wayne, Nebraska, and at Northeast Community College in Norfolk, Nebraska, where she also serves as the coordinator of the Visiting Writers Series and is the faculty editor of Northeast Community College's annual *Voices Out of Nowhere*.

www.ingramcontent.com/pod-product-compliance
Lightning Source LLC
Chambersburg PA
CBHW030050100426
42734CB00038B/1074